INUIT

Big Buddy Books

An Imprint of Abdo Publishing
abdopublishing.com

Katie Lajiness

abdopublishing.com

Published by Abdo Publishing, a division of ABDO, PO Box 398166, Minneapolis, Minnesota 55439.
Copyright © 2017 by Abdo Consulting Group, Inc. International copyrights reserved in all countries. No part
of this book may be reproduced in any form without written permission from the publisher. Big Buddy Books™
is a trademark and logo of Abdo Publishing.

Printed in the United States of America, North Mankato, Minnesota.
062016
092016

Cover Photo: © Ton Koene/Visuals Unlimited/Corbis; Shutterstock.
Interior Photos: © Corbis (p. 13); © Sue Flood/NPL/Minden Pictures (p. 15); *Getty Images*: Doug Allan (p. 29);
    © Igor Golovnov /Alamy (p. 27); © iStockphoto.com (p. 30); © NativeStock.com/AngelWynn (pp. 5, 9, 11, 16,
    17, 19); © NativeStock/North Wind Picture Archives (p. 21); © Michael Nolan/robertharding/Corbis (p. 25);
    © North Wind Picture Archives/Alamy (p. 26); © Patrick Pleul/dpa/Corbis (p. 23).

Coordinating Series Editor: Tamara L. Britton
Graphic Design: Adam Craven

Library of Congress Cataloging-in-Publication Data

Lajiness, Katie, author.
    Inuit / Katie Lajiness.
Minneapolis, MN : ABDO Publishing Company, 2017. | Series:
    Native Americans
LCCN 2015050491 | ISBN 9781680781991 (print) | ISBN 9781680774948 (ebook)
LCSH: Inuit--History--Juvenile literature. | Inuit--Social life and
    customs--Juvenile literature.
LCC E99.E7 L258 2017 | DDC 971.9004/9712--dc23
LC record available at http://lccn.loc.gov/2015050491

CONTENTS

Amazing People

Hundreds of years ago, North America was mostly wild, open land. Native American tribes lived on the land. They had their own languages and **customs**.

The Inuit (IH-noo-wuht) are one Native American tribe. They are known for living in cold, snowy regions and hunting seals and walrus. Let's learn more about these Native Americans.

Did You Know?

The name *Inuit* means "the people."

4

The Inuit wear parkas made from animal furs. Sometimes, they decorate their parkas with feathers and beads.

5

INUIT TERRITORY

Around 10,000 BC, the Inuit lived in Siberia, a large area in Russia. Over time, they spread across the Arctic. The Inuit settled in what is now Alaska in the United States, Canada, Greenland, and Russia.

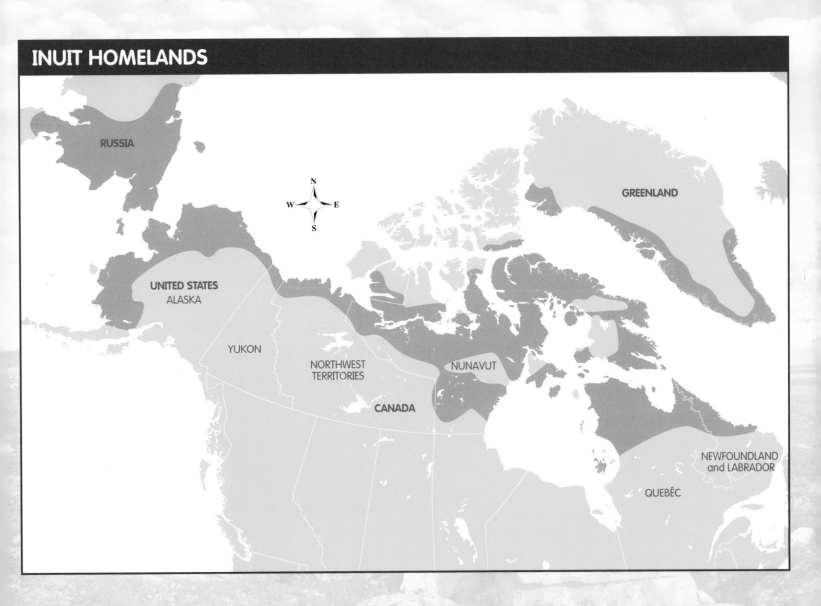

HOME LIFE

Inuit families had both summer and winter homes. In the summer, they lived in tents made from animal skins. To build winter homes, Inuit dug into the hillside with rocks and whalebones.

Depending on the weather, the Inuit changed how they traveled. During the warmer months, the Inuit walked or used **kayaks**. They rode dogsleds in the winter.

The Inuit built homes in the earth. The men covered them with dirt, grass, rocks, or wood.

What They Ate

The Inuit lived in cold areas where most fruit and vegetable crops could not grow. During the summer, they gathered berries, nuts, plants, and roots to eat. But meat made up much of their diets.

Inuit men were skilled hunters and fishermen. The Inuit ate fish, reindeer, seal, walrus, and whale. Meat was often eaten frozen or raw. When the Inuit cooked meat, they used soapstone pots.

Inuit seal hunters used boats made from wood and covered with animal skins. The hunter at the front of the boat used a harpoon to catch the seals.

Many Inuit ate fish-head soup. They used fish heads, fish tails, and seawater to make the soup.

Daily Life

Most Inuit lived in small groups near water. Families included a married couple and their children. Sometimes, their in-laws also lived with the group.

To keep warm, families needed warm clothing. So, men and women wore clothes made of animal skin or fur. Caribou, foxes, polar bears, and seals were popular choices. Their outfits included a parka, pants, socks, boots, and mittens.

Women carried young children in the back or hood of their parka.

In Inuit **culture**, people had different jobs. Men hunted and built hunting tools. They made **kayaks** and sleds, too. Women cooked meals and sewed clothes. Children learned these skills from their parents and the community.

Inuit women chewed leather to soften it for sewing.

15

Made by Hand

The Inuit made many objects by hand. They often used natural materials. These arts and crafts added beauty to everyday life.

Harpoons
Inuit men made the head of their harpoons with walrus tusks or whalebone. They used the harpoons to hunt animals.

Ulu Knives

Ulu (OO-loo) knives were made from stone. This tool had a rounded shape with a wood, bone, or ivory handle. Women used these knives to cut meat.

Boots

Women sewed boots from seal and caribou skin. These warm boots allowed people to move quietly while they hunted.

Snowshoes

Inuit women made snowshoes with a wooden frame and laces from animal skins.

17

Spirit Life

Inuit religion was based on nature. They honored animal spirits with **ceremonies** and **rituals** led by **shamans**. Sometimes the Inuit sang songs or wore wooden masks and charms. They believed certain songs and charms would help men during the hunt.

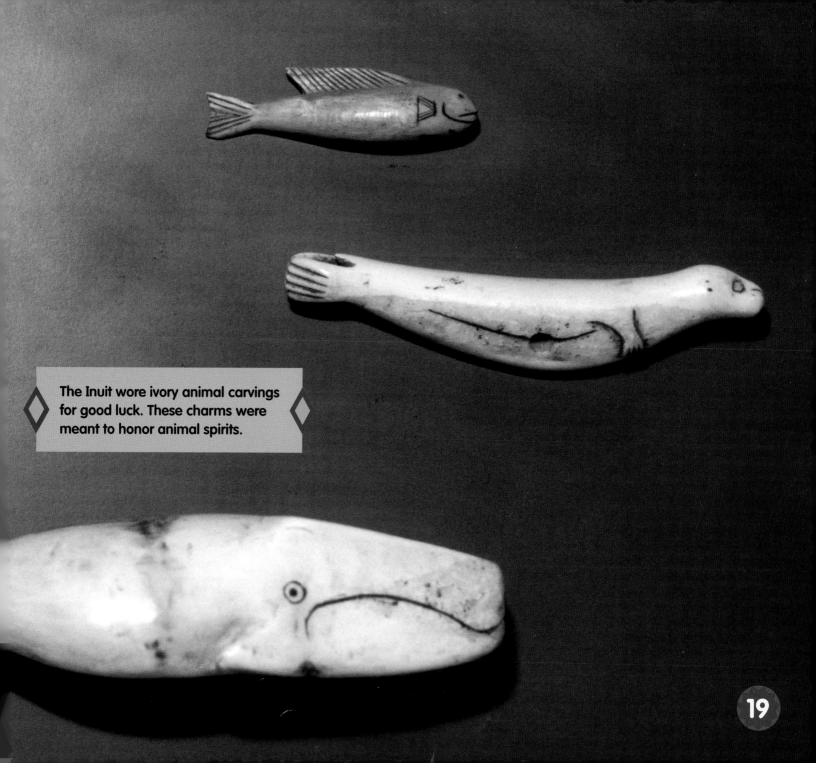

The Inuit wore ivory animal carvings for good luck. These charms were meant to honor animal spirits.

Storytellers

The Inuit told stories to teach about nature, values, and religion. Men danced as a way to tell hunting stories.

Inuit stories were about trouble between opposites. Light and dark or winter and summer were common subjects. Stories were popular during the winter. Sometimes, storytellers drew pictures in the snow with a knife.

The Inuit decorated ivory *(shown)*, bone, and horns as a way to tell stories.

Changing with the Times

In the 1500s, European fishermen sailed to Newfoundland and Labrador, Canada. There, they taught the Inuit to use metal tools.

In the 1700s and 1800s, **missionaries** visited the Inuit. They led many Inuit to become **Christians**. In the 1900s, Inuit who lived in English-speaking countries were forced to learn the language.

Moravian missionaries came to Greenland to convert the Inuit to Christianity. When Inuit left their villages, they left behind their churches.

23

Life for Inuit in the Arctic region continued to change. In 1939, the Canadian government took control of the Inuit who were living in Canada. The Inuit were forced to live in modern **reservations**.

Over time, the Inuit lifestyle changed. They traveled more by snowmobile and motorboat. Dogsleds and **kayaks** were used less often.

Modern life brought still more changes to the Inuit. Many began to receive health care and education. And, some began working for wages rather than living off the land.

Today, Inuit in the polar region of Greenland live in modern homes.

BACK IN TIME

1000

The first Europeans met the Inuit in what is now Newfoundland.

984

The Vikings met the Inuit in Greenland.

1576

British explorer Martin Frobisher met Inuit in northern Canada.

1741

Russian explorer Vitus Bering met the Inuit in Alaska.

Mid-1800s

Some Inuit worked and traded with sailors on whaling ships. The Inuit began using guns, wood, and iron, among other goods.

1999

The Inuit received a new homeland in Canada's Northwest Territories known as Nunavut.

THE INUIT TODAY

The Inuit have a long, rich history. They are remembered as skilled hunters and builders who lived in Arctic regions.

Inuit roots run deep. But the Inuit carry the **traditions**, stories, and memories of the past into the present. They keep alive the special things that make them Inuit.

Did You Know?

Today, about 160,000 Inuit live in Alaska, Canada, Greenland, and Russia.

Many modern Inuit continue to practice parts of their culture, such as dogsledding.

… For all the vital things
I had to get and to reach;
And yet there is only
one great thing,
The only thing,
To live to see the great
day that dawns
And the light that fills
the world.

– Anonymous (Inuit, 19th century)

GLOSSARY

ceremony a formal event on a special occasion.

Christian (KRIHS-chuhn) a person who practices Christianity, which is a religion that follows the teachings of Jesus Christ.

culture (KUHL-chuhr) the arts, beliefs, and ways of life of a group of people.

custom a practice that has been around a long time and is common to a group or a place.

kayak a portable boat.

missionary a person who travels to share his or her religious beliefs with others.

reservation (reh-zuhr-VAY-shuhn) a piece of land set aside by the government for Native Americans to live on.

ritual (RIH-chuh-wuhl) a formal act or set of acts that is repeated.

shaman a person who is believed to be able to use magic to heal sickness or see the future.

tradition (truh-DIH-shuhn) a belief, a custom, or a story handed down from older people to younger people.

WEBSITES

To learn more about Native Americans, visit **booklinks.abdopublishing.com**. These links are routinely monitored and updated to provide the most current information available.

INDEX